For Matteo, SS
For Vanessa and Mark, SN

First published in 2003 by Zero To Ten Limited
327 High Street, Slough, Berkshire, SL1 1TX
and 814 North Franklin Street, Chicago, Illinois 60610

Publisher: Anna McQuinn
Art Director: Tim Foster
Publishing Assistant: Vikram Parashar

A CIP catalogue record for this book is available from the British Library.

ISBN 1-84089-146-7

Let's look at
EYES

Written by
Simona Sideri

Illustrated by
Sheilagh Noble

Look at me, I use my eyes to see!

Eagles have excellent eyes!
They can spot their prey
from high in the sky.

Camels have bushy brows
that shade their eyes
from the burning, desert sun

They also have long eyelashes
to protect them from flying san

Owls don't move their eyes, so they always look as if they're staring.

Instead, they turn their heads right around to see in all directions!

Bushbabies can see in the dark.

They are nifty night hunters.

Lobsters' eyes are on
the end of little stalks.
They can peek out
    from behind rocks
        to check for danger.

Wasps have amazing eyes,
made up of many parts.

Each part of the eye
sees just a small part
of whatever they are looking at!

Eyes are excellent!